This Book
Belongs
To

Friendship's Offering

Techniques & Inspiration for Writing on Quilts

To Mary and Elly

We have been friends together
In sunshine and in shade.

Caroline Norton

Friendship's Offering

Techniques & Inspiration for Writing on Quilts

by Susan McKelvey

C&T PUBLISHING

Front and back covers
detail from *Puzzle Purse*
Susan McKelvey, 1987

All quilts by Susan McKelvey unless otherwise stated.

Copyright © 1990 by Susan McKelvey

Color and black and white photography by
Celia Pearson
Annapolis, Maryland

Edited by Nadene M. Hartley

Illustrations of section openings and calligraphy by
Susan Senesi
Annapolis, Maryland

Design and production by
Gillian Johnson
Gillian Johnson Studio
Annapolis, Maryland

Typesetting by
Best Impressions
Annapolis, Maryland
and
Typeworks
Hanover, Maryland

Published by
C & T Publishing
P.O. Box 1456
Lafayette, California 94549

ISBN: 0-914881-30-2

Library of Congress Catalog Card NO: 90-80501

Printed in Hong Kong

Contents

Thank You
for Kind Words Given

He that gives me small gifts would have me live.

George Herbert

When I reflect upon my years of collecting phrases of friendship, love and advice, I am filled with gratitude for all the contributions from quilting friends and students across the country. The gathering has been a labor of love (much more love than labor). In every class I have taught about writing on quilts, students have suggested designs to add to the repertoire of embellishments included here and have contributed beautiful sentiments they have either written or discovered.

This book truly has grown out of the endeavors of many. What more appropriate way to write a book about friendship and love than through this process of sharing and giving that echoes the best traditions of our quiltmaking forebears?

May you enjoy and use these phrases. And may we continue to collect, share, and exchange phrases of friendship, love and advice.

Remember the Past

*I desire no future that will break
the ties of the past.*

George Eliot

In the 19th century, album and friendship quilts reached great popularity. Both kinds were group projects and contained blocks contributed by many individuals. The quilts were often made as gifts to be presented to loved ones who were celebrating moves, marriages, anniversaries, or retirements. Album quilts were frequently competitive in spirit, with each block different, often original, and elaborately appliqued. Friendship quilts were both appliqued and pieced but were usually not competitive. Because both kinds of quilts were given as records of friendships and families, the blocks were usually signed. These signatures have provided a wealth of information and inspiration to today's quilt enthusiasts.

Album and friendship quilts were a part of the autograph fad of the era. Autograph books were popular, as were calling cards, cards de visite (calling cards with the newly-popular photographs of the callers on them), and gift cards such as Valentines and Christmas cards. Ladies' magazines of the period regularly provided sentimental phrases to be used in autograph albums and on quilts. Surviving autograph albums, usually signed by young ladies at academies, contain the same phrases we see on quilts. Good penmanship was taught, practiced, and honored, and the women and girls of the 19th century autographed everything with enthusiasm and grace.

The quotations, phrases and sentiments in this book have been collected from literature and from antique quilts, samplers, calling cards, and gift enclosures. When an author is known, the name is given. You should also give credit if you use the quotation. But many phrases have been in general use for centuries, stitched by young girls into their samplers, written into autograph books, and inked onto quilt blocks. They are well-known sentiments often seen in antique needlework. I have given sources when known so that you might see an actual sample or find more information.

When we examine 19th century album and friendship quilts, we see not only the signatures of the makers but beautifully inked drawings and medallions framing each name. The women used indelible ink to sign much of their handwork and to label their linens. They used the same ink to sign their quilts. The india ink used on the quilts has faded over the century to a sepia brown, but it has not been washed out. Many fine examples of the inked artwork of our quiltmaking forebears exist, and common elements run throughout these examples.

Because penmanship was taught and esteemed in the 1800's, many of the signatures we see on quilts of the time were beautifully written in a flowing script.

The signatures were frequently encased in inked medallions or tiny frames. These medallions were done in one of several ways. Tin stencils of border designs were available, and stencils could be custom made to include the quilters' signatures. Tin stamps were sometimes used to ink the medallions for the signatures. A third approach seemed to involve either an artistic member of the quilting group or a local artist hired to do the drawings. Freehand embellishments and even elaborate sketches abound on antique quilts just as they do in autograph albums of the period.

Although I admired and collected samples of the writing I saw on antique quilts, I did not incorporate it into my own work until 1987. Before then, the only writing I did on my quilts involved simply signing them. I tried signing them in many different ways: sometimes quilting, sometimes embroidering, sometimes writing with a permanent pen. But I used the pen with fear and trepidation because the pens then available were broad pointed and bled easily onto the fabric. My writing in no way resembled the delicate inkings of my forebears. Still, I persisted.

The first time I used writing on a quilt as embellishment rather than simply as documentation was on my "Puzzle Purse" quilt, shown on the cover and on page 44. This quilt is based on a love token I found in a book entitled *Folk Hearts*. This love token, called a "puzzle purse" by historians, is a watercolor and inked paper valentine given by a young man to his love in the late 1700's. The paper was folded into a tiny square and, when unfolded, revealed a central watercolor surrounded by phrases of love. The paper had obviously been refolded many times because stains marked the fold lines. This paper love token called out to me to become a quilt. I knew immediately that on this quilt I would have to write in the elaborate antique style. The result is "Puzzle Purse," in which the stains of the puzzle folds are reproduced with tea dyeing.

The joy I experienced in writing on that quilt is difficult to explain. Although it was a statement of ownership, it was even more a step toward freedom. Once I had done it—actually dared to write on the front of a quilt—I realized it was easy and fun. It opened new possibilities of creativity to me. At first, because I was now using the writing as embellishment, I strove to use the cooperplate style I saw on antique quilts. As I worked, however, I began to believe that I should use my own signature; otherwise it wouldn't be recognizable as mine years later when my children and grandchildren compared it to my letters and papers.

Still, I wanted to reproduce the delicate, flowing writing that I admired on the quilts of the 19th century. I began to practice using my own writing, but I made it fancier by adding flourishes, tails, and curliques. I found easy ways to embellish my handwriting while still keeping it identifiably mine.

I began sharing these methods with other quilters. Women who entered my classes convinced they could never write beautifully learned that they could, and they left excited about the possibilities for writing on quilts. In these classes, we also practiced drawing the medallions and pictures we admired. We found simple techniques for replicating them. As better pens became available, we were able to achieve fine, delicate lines like the inkings on antique quilts.

Because these techniques were developed by non-artists, we can all learn and use them. They are presented on the following pages for your perusal. Although we have never been taught ornate lettering, we can easily learn ways to embellish our signatures so that they reflect the style of our 19th century predecessors. It is my hope that you will use these writing instructions to enhance the quilts you make. As you do, remember the women who went before us and the tradition they began over a century ago. They obviously hoped we would remember, as this quaint phrase found on a quilt made by Esther J. White attests:

This quilt behind me I will leave,
When I am in my silent grave,
That my dear friends may view it o're
And think of me when I'm no more.

Forget Me Not

Writing
and
Drawing
on
Quilts

While writing the very toil gives pleasure,
And the growing work glows with the writer's heart.

Ovid

In this section are techniques for writing on fabric. If you follow the instructions step-by-step and allow yourself practice time before actually writing on a precious quilt, you will be able to achieve a writing style reminiscent of the 19th century inkings found on album and friendship quilts.

Supplies Needed

For writing on quilts:

- ◆ Permanent pens
  Any color or many colors
  Fine point
  Suggestions:
  Pigma SDK point 01-05
  Niji Stylist Permanent II

For marking the marking guide:

- ◆ Permanent pen
  Any color
  Thick point
  Suggestions:
  Sanford's Marker
  Design Art Marker

Fabric:

- ◆ 100% cotton works best. There is less bleeding than with polyester blends.
- ◆ Always prewash your fabric—the sizing on new fabric sometimes resists the ink
- ◆ Muslin for practice, any scraps
- ◆ Muslin: a 14″ square for the marking guide
- ◆ Flannel: an 18″ square (white) for the flannel board

Flannel Board:

- ◆ Matt board or foam core, a 14″ square

Equipment Needed

Fabric

You may choose any fabric which is light enough so the ink will show. However, 100% cotton works best for beginning experiments because there is usually more bleeding with polyester blends than with cottons. Always prewash your fabric before writing on it to eliminate the sizing which may act as a barrier to ink absorption. Most importantly, always test the particular fabric with the pen you are going to use. Test it for bleeding and washability before you invest hours of your time into the project.

Pens

A permanent pen is the first important piece of equipment you need in order to write on quilts. Although many pens are on the market, I have found two to be particularly useful. Both have been developed since I began writing on quilts only a few years ago, so I am sure improvements will be made and more pens will become available as we create a demand. Stay on the lookout for new pens and new colors to try.

Pens come in various point sizes. The lower the number, the finer the point. The pens used on the quilts shown range from the finest 005 through the broadest 05.

The Pigma SDK

The Pigma SDK is a wonderful pen for writing on fabric. The 01 makes a line as fine as any we see on antique quilts. The Pigma doesn't bleed, even if it is held in place. It's ideal for drawing. Because the point is so fine, you must write slowly, taking time to form the letters. This is the only adaptation you need to make in order to get good lettering from the Pigma. The ink is waterproof and acid free.

The Pigma SDK comes in a variety of colors, including black, brown, red, green, blue, rose, orange, and purple. Some of the colors come in several point sizes, too. The brown is my favorite color for imitating the sepia of the faded India ink on old quilts. It is a rusty shade, just right for an antique look.

The Niji Stylist II

Another pen which I have found to work well on fabric is the Niji Stylist II Permanent. It, too, comes in a variety of point sizes.

The black is a more intense black than the Pigma, and I use it when I want a darker color but still need a fine line. This pen bleeds more than the Pigma, especially if left in one place on the fabric, so you can and must write faster with it than with the Pigma. The Niji is good for inexperienced writers who want to write on fabric as they do on paper. Therefore, it is good for sending to relatives you want to sign pieces of fabric or quilt blocks. It is also good for a project in which you want a bolder, darker line. Again, I love to use the brown to achieve the faded antique look. The Niji brown is a rich chocolate and beautifully supplements the rust of the Pigma.

Testing The Pens For Bleeding

Always test every fabric with the pen you want to use. Pens react differently to each fabric. Before you begin, be sure you have the right pen for the job.

Washing Fabric You Have Written On

I have experimentally washed, and even soaked, sample inkings done with all the pens I use and have had no fading. I have tried name brand detergents in cold and warm water. The Pigma lines are so fine that the ink barely penetrates the fabric. It seems to need a day to set before it is completely permanent.

You must always wash quilts with writing on them just as you do any fine quilt: infrequently and only when absolutely necessary. Use a delicate detergent made especially for quilts. Wash by hand in the bathtub, keeping the quilt flat. Follow the detergent directions, which usually tell you to soak briefly without agitation, rinse, and lay flat to dry. Using these guidelines, I have had no problem with the ink washing out.

Anchoring Your Fabric

When you write on fabric, you need some way to anchor it so it doesn't slip. There are several possible ways to do this. The easiest is to tape down the corners of the fabric onto any work surface. This is quick, but the fabric can still slip.

A better way to prevent slipping is to iron the piece of fabric onto freezer paper. This stiffens the fabric for a better writing surface, but it is easily peeled off later. The freezer paper method has particular advantages if you are mailing fabric to others to write on and can't control how they will anchor the fabric. It insures that they will write smoothly. When you get the signed fabric back, just remove the freezer paper.

For those of you who are going to get involved in writing on fabric and try the exercises in this volume, I recommend making a flannel board. Make this by wrapping an 18″ piece of white flannel around a 14″ sheet of matt board or foam core (both available at any art supply store). You may make your flannel board any size, but the 14″ board has proven to be adequate yet not cumbersome. I originally designed the flannel board to carry the minute pieces of elaborate blocks from my cutting table to the sewing machine. I have found it equally useful for anchoring fabric on which I write. It also acts as a foundation for what I call the "marking guide." The marking guide provides guidelines for writing and drawing on fabric without drawing these guidelines directly on the final fabric.

How To Make A Marking Guide

This is a useful and easy-to-make piece of equipment for anyone who is going to write on fabric. You may make many different ones, depending upon your needs for a particular project. Simply take a piece of muslin any size (start with a 14″ square for the first one), and mark the guidelines with a DARK, THICK MARKER. You want the lines thick and heavy so they may be seen easily through your good fabric.

A line guide will be the first one you make. It will give you straight lines to follow when you are writing multi-lined quotations or quilt labels. Space your lines any distance apart. I usually have a set ¼″ apart and one ½″ apart.

You may want circles, ovals, or hearts on your guide (you will learn how to use these later). Using the marking guide means that you don't have to mark any guidelines on your beautiful quilt. Simply lay your fabric over the guide, centering the lines wherever you wish, and write. Because you marked heavily, you can see the lines easily through the top fabric. This marking guide also acts as an anchor for your fabric. Put the marking guide over the flannel board. Then you have a firm writing board, anchored fabric, and easy-to-see lines.

Here is a suggested layout for your first marking guide:

Practicing

Practicing makes perfect. Always test every fabric with the pen you want to use. Do a rough draft of what you are going to write or draw on a piece of the same fabric.

Because writing on fabric is different from writing on paper, practice on the fabric you will use. You cannot press as hard on fabric, and, because fabric causes the pen to drag, you must write more slowly. But fabric is more forgiving of mistakes than paper and allows you to correct and fill in lines that don't satisfy you.

Go through the exercises on the following pages until you feel comfortable with your handwriting and the techniques explained. Use the ones that seem appropriate for your style and adapt or discard others. Have fun and remember as you practice:

Thence comes to us that ingenious art
of painting words and speaking to the eyes;
And by the differing form of figures traced,
To give color and form to thought.

Brébœuf

Adapting Your Signature

When signing a quilt, use your own signature so it is identifiable in years to come as your work. "But," you may protest, "my handwriting isn't good enough!" It is! With just a few simple additions and some practice, your signature can be as showy and flowing as those you've admired. Try embellishing it by following the simple suggestions below. Then practice on muslin until you have achieved the effect you want.

First, write your name on fabric as you normally do. Go a little more slowly than if you were writing a check. Examine the letters to see where you can add tails and curliques. The beginnings and ends of words are good places. Tails may go up or down, or they can flow into the next word. First, simply add the swirls to your already written word. The next time include the swirls as you write.

Some letters benefit from exaggerating their shapes:

Try fattening and emphasizing any letter. All letters with tails offer opportunities for flourishes:

One of the disappointments of the current pens available is that they don't have chiseled points which would give the varied-width lettering of calligraphy. To compensate, try this: after writing a word or phrase, go over one side of each letter once more with the pen. Just choose one side of most letters and draw over the line a second time. Don't draw another line and fill in, and don't go over the entire word; that simply makes heavier writing. This gives the writing a luxurious feeling while keeping it delicate.

Amy   Amy

After practicing your name, practice other words you want to write. By using the pen slowly, adding tails and curliques, emphasizing letters, and enlarging the dots over the "i"s, you will give your writing the feeling of the 19th century script. Also, try varying the proportions between capitals and lower case letters. Before writing any phrase or sentence, practice it.

Friendship   Friendship
Love   Love
Thee   Thee
Julie   Julie
Remember Me
Remember Me

Sample Flourishes For Letters

The letters below are meant to suggest ways you can embellish your letters. Try them as you practice writing the phrases.

Drawing Vines and Flowers

In all the drawings discussed in this section, remember that you are not striving to be an artist. If you are an artist, you will have already figured out many ways to draw on quilts. This section is intended for those of you who don't really think you can draw on quilts. You can! The trick to all of the techniques given here is to create the "illusion" or the "suggestion" of vines, leaves, and flowers. Because you are using a fine pointed pen, working on fabric (which is surprisingly forgiving), and drawing on such a tiny scale, you can easily create the suggestion of flowers with simple dots and dashes. Your finished design will look professional, but it will have been simple to do.

Vines

The "S" curve is the most useful shape you can master for drawing vines and flowers. Use it for all vines, flower stems, and bouquets. Overlap the "S" curves or continue them. They may be any size and don't need to match. Draw the lines lightly because they will be covered later with leaves and flowers. All of these variations are shown below.

OVERLAPPED   CONTINUED   CHANGING DIRECTIONS

Leaves

Add leaves to the vines by resting the pen on the fabric or drawing small dots. The leaves needn't be perfectly formed or look exactly like each other. They may be paired or alternate; they may touch the vines or not. Notice each of these methods in the samples below:

Flowers

Again, the suggestion is what counts. Use dots, small or large. Clusters of three or five look like flowers, six like grapes, singletons like buds. Draw right on top of the vines. Space flowers far apart or close together. Either way is effective.

Grape Vine Tendrils

The Pigma pen is perfect for these. The grape vine tendrils are drawn last, may be placed anywhere on the vines, and may go in any direction. They are delicate squiggles, basically a series of "e"s ᴄᴇᴜᴜ, done with a VERY LIGHT TOUCH. Just touch the fabric lightly with the Pigma pen at the vine and draw quickly away from the vine, ending by lifting the pen off the fabric.

Wheat

Wheat is drawn with a comma stroke. Hold the pen still for just a second at the starting place; then drag it off the fabric at the end. This gives a heavier dot at the base, tapering to a slender tip.

Lily of the Valley

For lilies of the valley, make a curve. Then hang tiny half circles or bells on it. These bells may be filled in with ink or left open, depending on their size and how they look to you. You may attach the bells to the single curve or draw little curves coming off the large curve and hang the bells from these.

Lily of the Valley Leaves

An "S" curve will do the trick. Overlap two curves, coming to points at both ends. Then shade one side of the leaf as if it is turned. Or draw one "S" curve, but have the crossing curve not quite match.

Cattails

Do these by drawing sausages on stems. For a clump of cattails together, use the lily of the valley leaves and make the cattails each a different height. Put low grass at the base of any cluster.

Grapes

Grapes are just clusters of tiny circles of any size attached at any point on a vine.

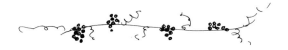

Grape Leaves

Grape leaves are fat and need to be drawn more accurately than the "suggestion" leaves we drew before. They are not necessary for the floral effect, however. Use them only if you feel comfortable with them.

Strawberries

Rose Buds

Violets

Bleeding Hearts

Roses in Bloom

Start with a bean shape . This becomes the outer petal. Then add smaller petals inside. Shade several. With the shading, the flower will look like a rose.

Antiquing and Shading

There are two ways to shade your drawings. Use dots—in corners, at folds, around the outside of medallions, at the corners of letters as in the example below.

Or use lines. This method is used primarily where ribbons or banners fold. Draw sketchy lines at folds to give dimension and to add shadow in the corners. Start your line at the drawn edge of the banner, lightening your touch at the end of the line as you did with the tendrils.

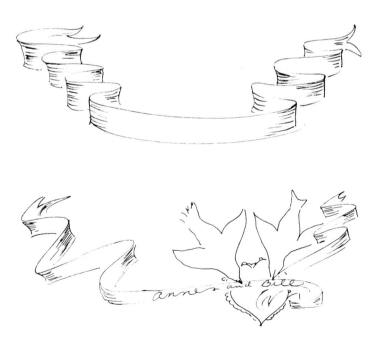

Making Your Own Medallions

One of the most exciting parts of writing and drawing on quilts is making your own medallions and wreaths in which to write your phrases of friendship, love or advice. Here is where the marking guide is useful. In order to avoid markings on your fabric, you add traceable shapes to the marking guide you designed at the beginning of this chapter. Any shape you want to make into a wreath can be drawn heavily on the marking guide.

Let's try a wreath first. Any round cup, plate or bowl will provide you with a circle. I have provided a small one here. Draw the circle on the marking guide with a thick, permanent pen. Lay your good fabric over the circle. Your circle should show through clearly. Using the circle as a guide, lightly draw vines around the circle. Remember, the vines need not match or be perfect. They will be covered up anyway. Start at the center top and draw the vines down on either side until they meet at the center bottom. You now have a perfect vine circle with no guide marks on your fabric. Decorate as you want. Put a thicker cluster of flowers and some dangling tendrils at the center top.

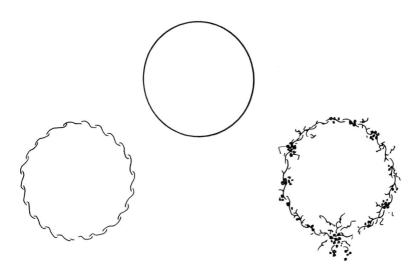

Use this method with any shape. Oval medallions provide plenty of room within them for writing. Always draw the shape on your marking guide first. Then trace with your vines, and your medallions will be perfect.

Medallions to Trace

Here are several medallions for you to trace and embellish. For each shape, I have provided the heavy, traceable line drawing on the left and shown a partially-decorated version on the right. Feel free to try different decorations each time you draw.

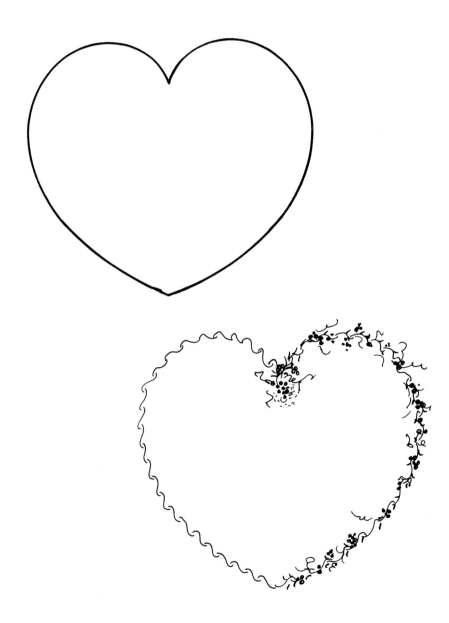

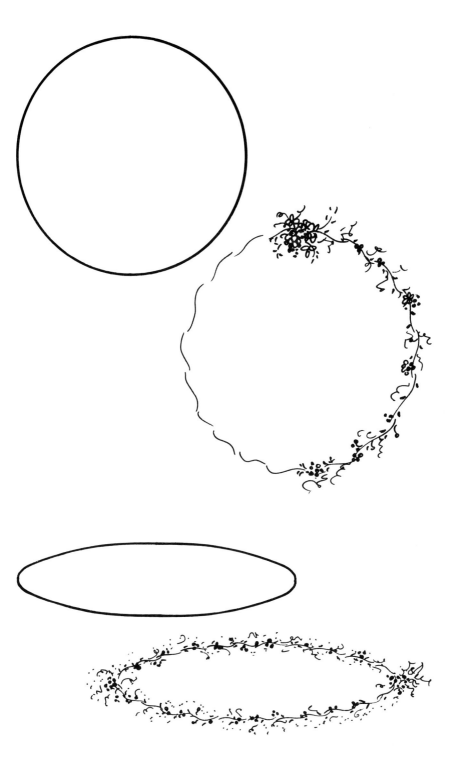

In my friend,
I find a second self

Phrases
of
Friendship

Friendship's Offering
Antique Quilt

A true friend is somebody who can make us do what we can.

Ralph Waldo Emerson

*Blessed are they who have the gift
  of making friends,
for it is one of God's best gifts.
It involves many things, but, above all,
the power of going out of one's self,
and appreciating whatever is noble
  and loving in another.*

Thomas Hughes
Needles and Friends

Love is but a moving shade,
Oft' changing with the sun;
Valued friendship ne'er will fade,
'Til our earthly course is run.

Needles and Friends

Friendship always benefits;
love sometimes injures.

Seneca

Happy is the house that shelters a friend.

Ralph Waldo Emerson

A friend hath the skill and observation
   of the best physician;
the diligence and vigilance of the best nurse;
and the tenderness and patience of the best mother.

Clarendon
Needles and Friends

"Friendship Quilt." 24" x 24". 1987. Hovering dove inspired by a design in *Spoken Without A Word*. Collection of Jackie and Bob Janovsky.

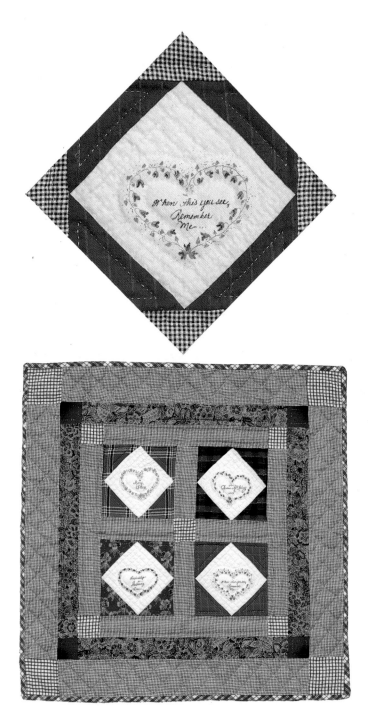

"Mary's Hearts." 21″ x 21″. 1989.
Collection of Mary & Tom Sharp.

Quilt labels from the "Remembrance Collection"
by Wallflower Designs.

"Album Applique." 52″ x 52″. Made by Susan McKelvey and
quilted by Cindy Yeoman. 1987. Author's collection.

"Encircled Heart." 39″ x 39″.
1988. Block designed by
Elly Sienkiewicz.

"Snowflake Medallion." 46″ x 46″. 1988. Inspired by a quilt
in *America's Glorious Quilts*. Author's collection.

Douglas
&
Susan

But for a being without end
the vow'd love we take
Grant us, oh God, one home
At last, For our Love's sake.

▪◂▸▪

1987

Detail of "Snowflake Medallion."

Antique Writing and Sewing Supplies:

Valentine, autograph album, tin stencils, enamel box, pens, scissors, calling cards, and signed quilt from the collection of the author. Metal stamps and letters, pearl needlecase, and darning ball from the collection of Nancy & Paul Hahn.

Antique 4″ doily.
1989.

"Anniversary Quilt." 36″ x 24″. 1987. Broiderie perse.
Collection of Karla and Kenneth Diaz.

"Wedding Quilt."
31″ x 31″. 1987.
Block and setting replicate
the Betsy Wright quilt in
Remember Me. Author's
collection.

"Puzzle Purse." 42″ x 42″. Inspired by 18th century love
token from *Folk Hearts*. Author's collection.

We made this quilt
For our dear Sue,
May her joys be many
And her sorrows few.

The Quilt Digest 4

A true friend is the greatest
   of all blessings,
And the one which we take the least
   thought to acquire.

La Rochefoucauld

Friendship either finds or makes equals.

Publilius Syrus

Your friend is the man who knows all about you
and still likes you.

Elbert Hubbard

Friendship's purposes preserved
May this forever be,
And as a mirror it will serve
To show thy friends to thee.

Quilted for Friends

What is a friend?
A single soul dwelling
in two bodies.

Aristotle

How much to be prized and esteemed is a friend,
On whom we may always with safety depend;
Our joys when extended will always increase,
And griefs when divided are hushed into peace.

Needles and Friends

Choose thy friends like thy books, few but choice.

James Howell

A true friend is forever a friend.

George Macdonald

The language of friendship is not words but meaning.

Henry David Thoreau

Friendship that flows from the heart cannot be frozen by adversity.

James Fenimore Cooper

*He that is thy friend indeed,
He will help you in your need.*

Shakespeare

If the while I think on thee, dear friend,
All losses are restored and sorrows end.

Shakespeare

Go oft' to the house of thy friend,
For weeds choke up the unused path.

Shakespeare

He who sows courtesy, reaps friendship,
And he who plants kindness,
*   gathers love.*

Needles and Friends

Wherever you are, it is your own friends who make your world.

William James

Into my quilts I stitch the memory of our friendship.

Roxy L. Burgard

A friend is the present you give yourself.

Robert Louis Stevenson

Friendship is a Sheltering Tree

Samuel Taylor Coleridge

Friendship redoubleth joys, And cutteth griefs in half.

Francis Bacon

49

We have been friends together
In sunshine and in shade.

Caroline Norton

A friend may well be reckoned
The masterpiece of nature.

Ralph Waldo Emerson

Friendship is the breathing rose,
With sweets in every fold.

Oliver Wendell Holmes

May the hinges of friendship never rust,
Or the wings of love lose a feather.

Edward Bannerman Ramsay

The only true gift is a portion
of yourself.

Ralph Waldo Emerson

A man must keep his friendship
in constant repair.

Samuel Johnson

Be slow in choosing a friend,
Slower in changing.

Benjamin Franklin

The only way to have a true friend is to be one.

Ralph Waldo Emerson

Without constancy there is neither love, friendship, nor virtue in the world.

Joseph Addison

Friendships multiply joys and divide griefs.

Henry George Bohn

If you have one true friend, you have more than your share.

Thomas Fuller

Phrases
of
Love

One who sleeps under a quilt
Is comforted by love.

Serene will be our days and bright,
And happy will our nature be,
When love is an unerring light,
And joy its own security.

William Wordsworth

Two souls in one, two hearts into one heart.

Du Bartas

Two souls with but a single thought,
Two hearts that beat as one.

Von Münch-Bellinghausen

Dawn love is silver,
Wait for the west:
  Old love is gold love —
  Old love is best.

Katherine Lee Bates

Age enricheth true love,
Like noble wine.

Gerald Massey

Chance cannot change my love,
nor time impair.

Robert Browning

True love is the ripe fruit of a lifetime.

Lamartine

They sin who tell us love can die.
With life all other passions fly,
All others are but vanity.

Robert Southey

True love in this differs from gold and clay,
That to divide is not to take away.

Shelley

May flowers of love
Around thee be twined,
And the sunshine of peace
Shed its joy o're thy mind.

Antique Valentine

Hands to Work,
And hearts to God.

Shaker Motto

Whom God has joined together,
Let no man put asunder.

Would that this garland fair
Might weave around thy life,
A spell to shield from care,
A guard from every strife.

Antique Valentine

Heart and Hand shall never part,
When this you see,
Remember Me.

Folk Hearts

None knew Thee but to Love Thee;
None named Thee but to praise.

Fitz-Greene Halleck

I will wear my heart upon my sleeve.

Shakespeare

Connected as the hand and glove,
Is, madam, poetry and love.

David Lloyd

Love looks not with the eyes,
But with the mind;
And therefore is winged Cupid
painted blind.

Shakespeare

Who ever loved that loved not at first sight?

Christopher Marlowe

Come live with me, and be my love,
And we will all the pleasures prove.

Christopher Marlowe

Silence in love betrays more love
Than words, though ne'er so witty.

Sir Walter Raleigh

Love can hope where reason would despair.

Lord Lyttelton

That which cometh from the heart
will go to the heart.

Jeremiah Burroughes

When Silence speaks for Love,
She has much to say.

Richard Garnett

To know, to esteem, to love,
And then to part,
Makes up life's tale to many
a feeling heart!

Samuel Taylor Coleridge

Love seeketh not itself to please,
Nor for itself hath any care.

William Blake

To thee only God granted
A heart ever new:
To all always open,
To all always true.

Matthew Arnold

All I know of love
Is that love is all there is.

Emily Dickinson

Lovers well know what grief it is to part,
For twixt two lovers' lives
is but one heart.

Folk Hearts

When two fond hearts as one unite,
The yoke is easy and the burden light.

Needles and Friends

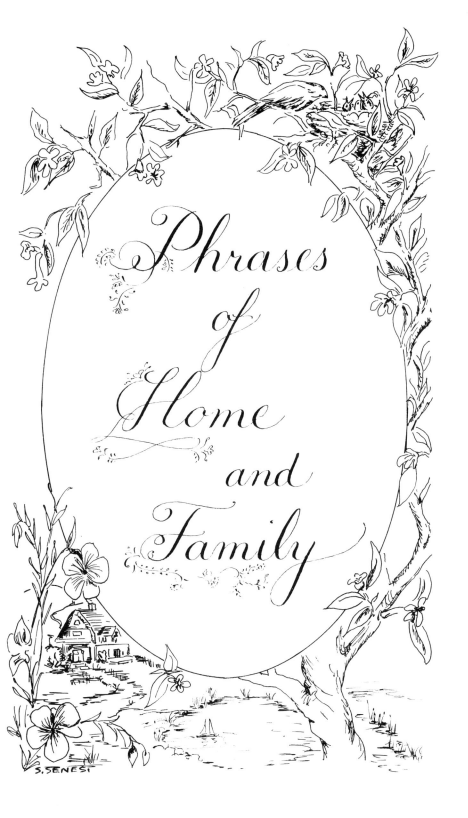

Phrases
of
Home
and
Family

S. SENESI

East and West, Home is best.

Charles Haddon Spurgeon

But wheresoe'er I'm doomed to roam,
I still shall say — that home is home.

William Combe

Be it ever so humble, there's no place like home.

John Howard Payne

His home, the spot of earth supremely blest,
A dearer, sweeter spot than all the rest.

James Montgomery

Home is where the heart is.

Pliny the Elder

Where we love is home.
Home that our feet may leave,
but not our hearts.

Oliver Wendell Holmes

But what on earth is half so dear —
So longed for — as the hearth of home?

Emily Brontë

But every house where Love abides
And Friendship is a guest,
Is surely home, and home, sweet home;
For there the heart can rest.

Henry Van Dyke

Old homes! old hearts! Upon my
    soul forever
Their peace and gladness lie
like tears and laughter.

Madison Julius Cawein

Blest be that spot, where cheerful
    guests retire
To pause from toil, and trim their
    evening fire;
Blest that abode, where want
    and pain repair,
And every stranger finds a
    ready chair.

Oliver Goldsmith

Children have more need of
models than critics.

Joseph Joubert

A mother is a mother still,
The holiest thing alive.

Samuel Taylor Coleridge

The childhood shows the man,
As morning shows the day.

John Milton

Train up a child in the way he should go,
And when he is old he will never depart
from it.

Proverbs 22:6

The mother's heart is the child's schoolroom.

Henry Ward Beecher

Between the dark and the daylight,
When the night is beginning to lower,
Comes a pause in the day's occupations
That is known as the children's hour.

Henry Wadsworth Longfellow

We need love's tender lesson taught
As only weakness can;
God hath His small interpreters,
The child must teach the man.

John Greenleaf Whittier

The child is the father of the man.

William Wordsworth

God cannot be everywhere,
So He made mothers.

With Thanks and Appreciation

Delightful task! To rear the tender thought.
To teach the young idea how to shoot.

James Thompson

I remember, I remember
    How my childhood fleeted by, —
The mirth of its December,
    And the warmth of its July.

Winthrop Mackworth Praed

Just as the twig is bent the tree's inclined.

Alexander Pope

Respect the child.
Be not too much his parent.
Trespass not on his solitude.

Ralph Waldo Emerson

Phrases
of
Giving

Affection's Offering

Absent but Dear

A Token of Affection

The greatest grace of a gift, perhaps, is that it anticipates and admits of no return.

Henry Wadsworth Longfellow

Though small the gift to thee I send,
Acceptance let it meet,
For even trifles from a friend
In friendship's eyes are sweet.

With Thanks and Appreciation

The gift is small,
But love is all.

Needles and Friends

Accept this trifle that I send,
Not as a stranger, but as a friend.

Remember Me

Accept, my friend, this little pledge,
Your love and friendship to engage,
If 'ere we should be called to part,
Let this be settled in your heart,
That when this little piece you see,
You ever will remember me.

Remember Me

Not what we give,
But what we share,
For the gift without the giver
Is bare.

James Russell Lowell

A heart I send you,
    Squire Baldwine,
Reject it not, I do implore thee.
A warm reception may it meet,
My name a secret I must keep.

Folk Hearts

Phrases
of
Remembrance

S.SENESI

Praising what is lost
Makes the remembrance dear.

Shakespeare

When this you see,
Remember me,
Though many a mile
We distant be.

Needles and Friends

When I am dead and in my grave,
When all my bones are rotten,
When this you see, Remember me,
That I may not be forgotten.

Quilted for Friends

This quilt behind me I will leave,
When I am in my silent grave,
That my dear friends may view it o're,
And think of me when I'm no more.

Forget Me Not

When this you see,
Remember Me.

Remember Me

The heart has its own memory,
   like the mind,
And in it are enshrined
The precious keepsakes, into which
   is wrought
The giver's loving thought.

Henry Wadsworth Longfellow

The memories we collect and give,
brighten our lives as long as we live.

Julie Sneyd

A place in thy memory, Dearest!
Is all that I claim:
To pause and look back when thou hearest
The sound of my name.

Gerald Griffin

Phrases
of
Advice

Friendship's Offering

Gather ye rosebuds while ye may.

Robert Herrick

*I desire no future that will break the ties
of the past.*

George Eliot

*Yesterday is already a dream,
And tomorrow is only a vision;
but today well-lived makes every yesterday
A dream of happiness
And every tomorrow a vision of hope.*

The Sanskrit

*Success is knowing that because of you the world
is a little better.*

Michael Sneyd

Save the Pieces
Remember Me

Deal justly and love many.
Remember Me

Lives of great men remind us,
We can make our lives sublime;
And, departing, leave behind us,
Footprints on the sands of time.

Henry Wadsworth Longfellow

Be thou the rainbow to the storms of life.

Lord Byron

Happy the man, and happy he alone,
He who can call today his own:
He who, secure within, can say:
Tomorrow, do thy worst, for I have
     lived today.

John Dryden

There's a destiny that makes us brothers.
None goes his way alone.
All that we send into the lives of others,
Will come back into our own.

Edwin Markham

Do what you can
With what you have
Where you are.

Theodore Roosevelt

Many hands make light work.

Old English Proverb, 1460

*The journey of a thousand miles
Begins with one step.*

Lao-tse

*Life can only be understood backwards;
but it must be lived forwards.*

Soren Kierkegaard

*We live in deeds, not years, in thoughts,
    not breaths,
In feelings, not in figures in a dial.
We should count time by heart-throbs,
He most lives who thinks most,
    feels noblest, acts the best.*

Phillip James Bailey

To every thing there is a season,
And a time for every purpose under
the heavens.

Ecclesiastes 3:1

Look toward the Sun,
And the shadows will fall behind you.

Sundial in Rye, Sussex, England

A thing of beauty is a joy forever:
Its loveliness increases;
It will never pass into nothingness.

John Keats

No one is useless in this world
Who lightens the burdens of it
for another.

Charles Dickens

Slight not what's near,
Through aiming at what's far.

Euripides

Whatsoever thy hand findeth to do,
Do it with thy might.

Ecclesiastes 9:10

No man is an island entire of itself;
every man is a piece of the continent,
a part of the main.

John Donne

Pleasant words are like a honeycomb,
Sweetness to the soul and health to the body.

Proverbs 16:24

This above all: to thine own self be true,
And it must follow as the night the day,
Thou canst not then be false to
   any man.

Shakespeare

The woods would be very silent if no birds sang
there except those who sang best.

John James Audubon

The years teach much which the days
never know.

Ralph Waldo Emerson

To create a little flower is the labor
of ages.

William Blake

Bibliography

Bartlett, John. *Bartlett's Familiar Quotations.* Boston: Little, Brown and Co., 1980.

Bickham, George. *The Universal Penman.* (Originally published by George Bickham, London, circa 1740-41.) New York: Dover, 1954.

Binny, Edward, and Gail Binny-Winslow. *Homage to Amanda.* San Francisco: R K Press, 1984.

Duke, Dennis, and Deborah Harding. *America's Glorious Quilts.* New York: Park Lane, 1987.

Ferraro, Pat, Elaine Hedges, and Julie Silber. *Hearts and Hands.* San Francisco: The Quilt Digest Press, 1987.

Kile, Michael, *The Quilt Digest 4.* San Francisco: The Quilt Digest Press, 1986.

Kolter, Jane Bentley. *Forget Me Not.* Pittstown, N.J.: Main Street Press, 1985.

Lasansky, Jeannette. *In the Heart of Pennsylvania.* Lewisburg, Pa.: Oral Traditions Project, 1985.

----------. *Pieced by Mother.* Lewisburg, Pa.: Oral Traditions Project, 1987.

Lipsett, Linda Otto. *Remember Me.* San Francisco: The Quilt Digest Press, 1985.

May-Levenick, Denise. *Needles and Friends.* Pasadena, Calif.: Levenick, 1983.

McKelvey, Susan. "Writing on Quilts." *Traditional Quiltworks,* Feb-April, 1989, pp. 42-43.

Nicoll, Jessica F. *Quilted by Friends.* Winterthur, Del: The Henry Francis du Pont Winterthur Museum, 1986.

Ohrbach, Barbara Milo. *A Token of Friendship.* New York: Clarkson N. Potter, 1987.

Ross, Pat. *With Thanks and Appreciation.* New York: Viking Penguin, 1989.

Schaffner, Cynthia V.S., and Susan Klein. *Folk Hearts.* New York: Alfred A. Knopf, 1984.

Sienkiewicz, Elly. *Baltimore Beauties and Beyond.* Lafayette, Calif.: C & T Publishing, 1989.

——————. *Spoken Without a Word.* Washington, D.C.: Turtle Hill Press, 1983.

Stevenson, Burton. *The Home Book of Quotations.* New York: Dodd Mead & Co., 1967.

Credits

The quotations, phrases and sentiments in this book have been collected from literature, quilts, and antique items such as samplers, calling cards, and gift enclosures. When an author is known, the name is given. You should also give credit if you use the quotation. Many phrases have been in general use for centuries, stitched by young girls into their samplers, written into autograph books, and inked onto quilt blocks. They are well-known sentiments seen often in antique needlework.

Some of the quotations appeared on quilts and other folk art pictured in books listed in the Bibliography. The photographs of these pieces may be of great interest to you. Therefore, we recommend the books as authoritative sources on original antique phrases and handwriting.

We have made every effort to trace the copyright holders of phrases in this book. We apologize to any who have been inadvertently omitted and would appreciate hearing from you.

We wish to thank the following for permission to use phrases or designs from works in copyright:

Dr. Irwin Berman; Quilt from Linda and Irwin Berman Children's Quilt Collection, Baltimore Museum of Art, Baltimore, Maryland.

Denise May-Levenick Designs; *Needles and Friends* edited by Denise May-Levenick. Copyright © 1983.

Hugh Lauter Levin Associates, Inc.; *America's Glorious Quilts* by Dennis Duke and Deborah Harding. Copyright © 1987.

Sources and Suppliers

Ask your local quilt shop, art supply store, or bookstore for permanent pens, Victorian patterns, and the books listed in the Bibliography.

All recommended writing supplies plus "The Remembrance Collection" of Silkscreened Medallions and Patterns are available from Wallflower Designs, 1573 Millersville Road, Millersville, Maryland 21108. (Send $1.50 for catalogue).

Write for a free catalog of other fine quilting books from
    C & T Publishing
    P.O. Box 1456
    Lafayette, CA 94549

About the Author

Susan McKelvey is a quilter, English teacher, and the owner of Wallflower Designs. She is the author of *Color for Quilters, The Color Workbook,* and *Light and Shadows.* She resides in Anne Arundel County, Maryland, with her husband, Douglas, and their two children, Leslie and Scott.

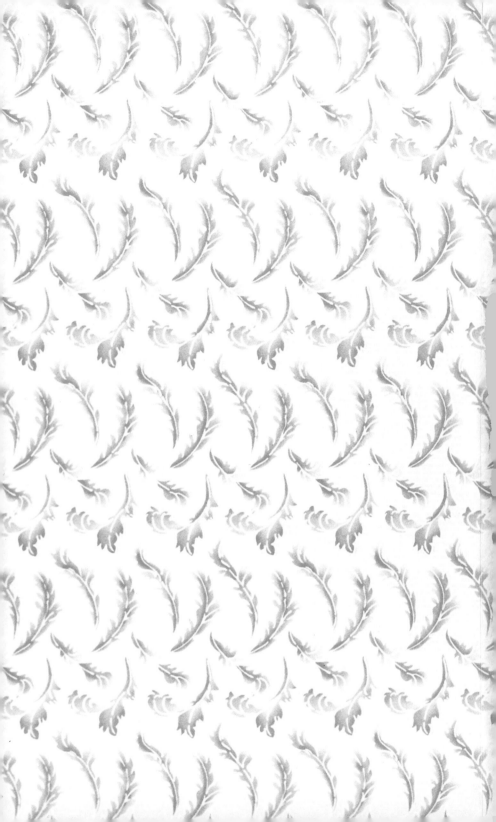